Driving in the City

Donna Montgomery

Illustrated by Klebs Junior

OXFORD
UNIVERSITY PRESS

198 Madison Avenue
New York, NY 10016 USA

Great Clarendon Street, Oxford ox2 6DP UK

Oxford University Press is a department of the
University of Oxford. It furthers the University's
objective of excellence in research, scholarship,
and education by publishing worldwide in

Oxford   New York
Auckland Cape Town Dar es Salaam
Hong Kong Karachi Kuala Lumpur Madrid
Melbourne Mexico City Nairobi New Delhi
Shanghai Taipei Toronto

With offices in

Argentina Austria Brazil Chile Czech Republic
France Greece Guatemala Hungary Italy Japan
Poland Portugal Singapore South Korea
Switzerland Thailand Turkey Ukraine Vietnam

OXFORD and OXFORD ENGLISH are registered
trademarks of Oxford University Press.

© Oxford University Press 2009

Database right Oxford University Press (maker)

Any websites referred to in this publication are in
the public domain and their addresses are provided
by Oxford University Press for information only.
Oxford University Press disclaims any responsibility
for the content.

Executive Publishing Manager: Stephanie Karras
Managing Editor: Sharon Sargent
Design Manager: Stacy Merlin
Project Coordinator: Sarah Dentry
Production Layout Artist: Colleen Ho
Cover Design: Colleen Ho, Stacy Merlin,
Michael Steinhofer
Manufacturing Manager: Shanta Persaud
Manufacturing Controller: Eve Wong

ISBN: 978 0 19474031 9 (BOOK)

ISBN: 978 0 19474039 5 (OPD READING LIBRARY)

ISBN: 978 0 19474057 9 (CIVICS READING LIBRARY)

Printed in China

10 9 8 7

Many thanks to Pronk&Associates, Kelly Stern,
and Meg Brooks for a job well done.

Driving in the City

Table of Contents

Before **Reading**

A. Match the pictures with the words.

___d__ 1. DMV clerk

_____ 2. DMV handbook

_____ 3. driver's license

_____ 4. expiration date

_____ 5. license plate

_____ 6. proof of insurance

_____ 7. registration sticker

_____ 8. testing area

_____ 9. vision exam

2

B. Answer the questions.

1. Do you need a car? Why or why not?
2. What driving rules do you know?
3. Why do people go to the Department of Motor Vehicles?

C. Read the title of this book. Look at the pictures in the book. Then guess the answers to the questions. Circle *a* or *b*.

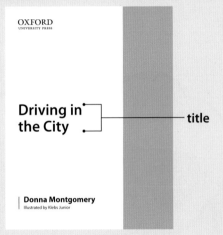

OXFORD
UNIVERSITY PRESS

Driving in
the City ————————— title

Donna Montgomery
Illustrated by Klebs Junior

1. What are you going to read about in this book?
   a. riding a bicycle
   b. driving a car

2. What kind of test is in Chapter 3?
   a. a driving test in a car
   b. a written driving test

3. Where does Miguel live?
   a. in a big city
   b. in a small town

Chapter 1

New Places, New Needs

This is my new apartment in Los Angeles. I moved here from a small town. In that town, I always rode my bike. Here I can't do that because places are too far away from one another. I need a car. I also need to learn to drive and to get a driver's license. I'm confused. What should I do first? I call my friend William and ask for his help.

William answers the phone. "Hello," he says.

I say, "Hi, William. This is Miguel. Can you come to my apartment today?"

"Sure," William says. "Why do you want me to come?"

"I'm very confused! I have some questions, and I need your help," I answer.

"No problem," says William. "I can be there in about half an hour."

"That's great! See you later," I say.

William arrives, and we shake hands. He comes into my apartment. He asks, "Do you want me to unpack all of these big boxes?"

"No!" I laugh. "I need help, but I can unpack the boxes. I need a driver's license and a car. I also want to learn how to drive. I don't know where to start."

"Oh, I can help you! I moved here from Toronto, and I had the same problem," William says.

"The first thing you need is a DMV handbook," says William. "It has all of the driving rules."

I ask, "Where can I get one of those books?"

"At the DMV," William says.

"Is the DMV a bookstore?" I ask.

"No," William answers. "It's the Department of Motor Vehicles."

He drives me to the DMV, and I pick up a handbook there. I'm glad William is my friend.

California Driver Handbook

Reading Check

A. Choose the correct answer.

1. Miguel moved to Los Angeles from ____ .
   - **a.** a small town
   - **b.** a big city
   - **c.** Toronto

2. Miguel asks William to help him ____ .
   - **a.** unpack boxes
   - **b.** find a bookstore
   - **c.** get a driver's license

3. At the DMV, Miguel gets ____ .
   - **a.** a driver's license
   - **b.** a book about driving rules
   - **c.** information about buying a car

B. Complete the sentences. Use the words in the box.

apartment	~~confused~~	DMV handbook
driver's license	glad	unpack

1. There are a lot of rules. I'm _____confused_____ .
2. I moved into a new house. I need to _____ boxes.
3. The driving rules are in the _____ .
4. I use my _____ as ID.
5. When you pass a test, you feel _____ .
6. An _____ is a type of home.

C. Understand cause and effect. Circle the correct answer.

1. Why does Miguel need a car now?
   a. because he lives in a small town now
   b. because he lives in a big city now
   c. because he doesn't like riding his bike

2. Why does Miguel need a DMV handbook?
   a. to find places in the city
   b. to learn about Los Angeles
   c. to learn the driving rules

3. Why is Miguel glad?
   a. because he has a good friend
   b. because he unpacked all his boxes
   c. because he passed his test

What's Next in Chapter 2?

What's going to happen next? What do you think? Circle your guess, *yes* or *no*.

1. Is Miguel going to take a driver education course?
   yes   no

2. Is William going to take a written driving test?
   yes   no

3. Is Miguel going to pass a written driving test?
   yes   no

Chapter 2

Rules and Practice

At home, I start reading the DMV handbook. There's a chapter about stop signs and other road signs. I know most of these signs! I have to obey them when I ride my bicycle. I also know some hand signals. I use them when I'm going to turn or stop. The things I know about bicycle and road safety can help me drive a car. I'm relieved.

The handbook has many rules about road safety and speed limits. There's a lot of information. How do you make left and right turns? How far should you park from a fire hydrant? I get confused. I'm going to take a driver education course.

Mr. Hall teaches the course. He teaches the students about signs, traffic lights, and seat belts. We also learn about parking areas and no-parking zones.

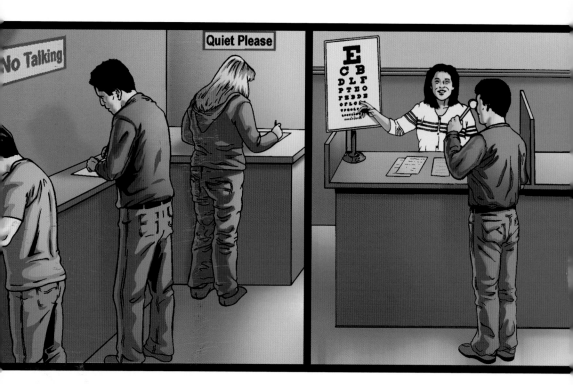

Today I go to the DMV. I'm going to take the written part of my driving test and a vision exam. When I go to the testing area, I'm nervous.

I take my test in the testing area. Then a DMV clerk checks the answers. After a few minutes, she gives me good news. I passed!

I pass the vision exam, too. The clerk gives me a learner's permit. Now I can learn to drive!

The next day, I start a driver's training course. I show my learner's permit to Mrs. Sato. She's my driving instructor. Mrs. Sato and I go to a car. It has a sign on top that says, "Student Driver."

I practice driving with Mrs. Sato every week. Parking is hard! Mrs. Sato says, "Don't worry. Most people have problems with parking."

After 15 lessons, I'm ready to take my driving test.

A. Mark the sentences T (true) or F (false).

__T__ 1. Miguel knows some of the information in the DMV handbook.

_____ 2. Miguel doesn't need a driver education course.

_____ 3. Miguel doesn't pass his written test.

_____ 4. Miguel needs a learner's permit for the driver's training
          course.

_____ 5. Miguel thinks parking is easy.

B. Complete the sentences. Use the words in the box.

DMV clerk	fire hydrant	relieved
testing area	traffic light	vision exam

1. Three people are taking the test in the _____ .

2. During a _____ , you read an eye chart.

3. A _____ gives you a learner's permit when you pass
   the written test.

4. She passed the test! She feels _____ .

5. You can't park next to a _____ .

6. He stops when the _____ turns red.

C. Understand cause and effect. Circle the correct answer.

1. Why does Miguel know some of the signs in the DMV handbook?
   a. He knows how to drive a car.
   b. He obeys the signs when he rides his bicycle.
   c. He teaches a driver's training course.

2. Why does Miguel take a driver education course?
   a. He doesn't understand all the information in the handbook.
   b. He wants to learn hand signals.
   c. He wants to teach driving classes.

3. Why does Miguel pass the written test?
   a. He guesses each answer.
   b. He knows the driving rules.
   c. He knows hand signals.

What's Next in Chapter 3?

What's going to happen next? What do you think? Circle your guess, *yes* or *no*.

1. Is Miguel going to take another written test?
   yes   no

2. Is Miguel going to have a problem during his test?
   yes   no

3. Is Miguel going to pass his driving test?
   yes   no

Chapter 3

The Big Test

I call William. "I finished the driver's training course," I say. "I also practiced my driving with an instructor. Now I'm ready for my driving test. I have an appointment for the test tomorrow at 12:30. Can you drive me to the DMV?"

"Sure," says William. "I can pick you up at noon. You can use my car for your test."

"Thanks a lot. You're a real friend!"

The next day, William and I walk into the DMV. I show the DMV clerk my learner's permit. I say, "I have an appointment for a driving test." She tells me to go to the waiting area.

In a few minutes, another DMV clerk calls my name. The clerk takes me outside, and I meet Mr. Ortiz. He's going to give me the driving test. He follows me to William's car.

Mr. Ortiz and I get into William's car. We put on our seat belts, and I start the car. Mr. Ortiz tells me where to drive and when to turn. I try to stay calm. I stop at all the stop signs and look both ways before I go on. I follow the speed limit signs. When we get back to the DMV, I park between two cones. Mr. Ortiz says, "Very good. You passed!"

I go back into the DMV. I'm excited.

"You passed!" says William. "I know because you're smiling. That's great!"

I hear a DMV clerk call my name. He takes my picture. Another clerk gives me a temporary license. The expiration date on it is 60 days from today. She says that my new driver's license is going to come in the mail before the expiration date.

William says, "You can drive my car home."

I feel very proud.

Reading Check

A. These sentences are false. Make them true.

1. Miguel has an appointment for a written test.

   <u>Miguel has an appointment for a driving test.</u>

2. Miguel drives over the speed limit.

3. Miguel parks between two cars.

4. Miguel looks sad after the driving test.

5. Miguel is going to get his temporary license in the mail.

B. Choose *a* or *b*.

1. You can't start driving without a ___ .
   a. learner's permit
   b. new car

2. Make an ___ with the doctor for a checkup.
   a. expiration date
   b. appointment

3. Don't be nervous about the test. You need to stay ___ .
   a. excited
   b. calm

4. My son got 96 percent on his exam. I'm very ___ of him.
   a. proud
   b. confused

5. The ___ on a driver's license shows when you need a new license.
   a. expiration date
   b. sign

C. Understand cause and effect. Match the two parts of each sentence.

<u>b</u> 1. Miguel passed the test because

2. William knows Miguel passed because

3. Miguel gets only a temporary license because

4. Miguel is proud because

a. he passed the test.

b. he's a good driver.

c. the new license is going to come in the mail.

d. Miguel is smiling.

What's Next in Chapter 4?

What's going to happen next? What do you think? Circle or write your guess.

1. What color car is Miguel going to buy?
   a. blue
   b. green
   c. red
   d. other: _____

2. How is Miguel going to find a car?
   a. by talking to William
   b. by going to a place that sells new cars
   c. by looking at newspaper ads
   d. other: _____

3. What is Miguel going to do after he buys a car?
   a. drive William home
   b. drive to work
   c. drive to the beach
   d. other: _____

Chapter 4

Buying a Car

"Okay, William," I say. "Now I need to buy a car." We look at the used-car ads in the newspaper. I point to a picture of a small car. It's red—my favorite color! We call the phone number in the ad. Then we go to see the car.

The car is in good condition, and it drives well, too. I like it a lot! I buy the car for a good price.

Now I have a driver's license and a car. I ask William, "What other things do I need?"

William answers, "You need car insurance. I can introduce you to my insurance agent. He can help you."

I talk to the insurance agent. Car insurance costs a lot! I'm surprised. I pay the fee, and I get a proof of insurance card. I'm going to keep the card in my car.

"There's one more thing to do," says William. "You need to go back to the DMV and register your car."

I ask, "How do I register my car?"

William answers, "You show that you're the owner of the car. You also show proof of insurance. After you pay a fee, you get registration stickers and license plates. You put them on your car."

"I have to pay again?" I ask. I don't have much money left!

William and I drive to the DMV in my car. I show the DMV clerk my insurance card and driver's license, and I pay the fee. Then the clerk gives me registration stickers and license plates for my car.

William says, "You need one more thing, but don't worry. You don't have to pay for it." He gives me a map of the city.

"Thanks!" I say. "Let's drive to the beach. The map can help us get there."

A. Circle the correct answer.

1. Where does Miguel buy his car?

    a. from a place that sells new cars
    b. from a place that sells used cars
    c. from the owner of the car

2. What does Miguel do first?

    a. get car insurance
    b. put license plates on his car
    c. register the car

3. What happens at the end of the story?

    a. Miguel doesn't have money for the registration fee.
    b. Miguel buys a map of the city.
    c. William gives Miguel a map of the city.

B. Choose *a* or *b*.

1. She was ⎯⎯ when her friends had a party for her.

    a. surprised
    b. calm

2. You get a ⎯⎯ of insurance card when you buy car insurance.

    a. permit
    b. proof

3. A ⎯⎯ goes on the back of a car.

    a. driver's license
    b. license plate

4. You put ⎯⎯ on your license plate.

    a. registration stickers
    b. a learner's permit

5. Where is the DMV? I need a ⎯⎯ .

    a. map
    b. fee

C. Understand cause and effect. Match the two parts of each sentence.

_____ 1. Miguel looks at newspaper ads because

_____ 2. Miguel talks to an insurance agent because

_____ 3. Miguel goes back to the DMV because

_____ 4. Miguel doesn't pay for the map because

a. William gives it to him.

b. he needs to register his car.

c. he needs car insurance.

d. he wants to buy a car.

What's Next?

What's going to happen next? What do you think? Circle your guess, _yes_ or _no_.

1. Are Miguel and William going to get lost on the way to the beach?

   yes   no

2. Is Miguel going to swim at the beach?

   yes   no

3. Are Miguel and William going to eat at the beach?

   yes   no

After Reading Activity

A. Read a map.

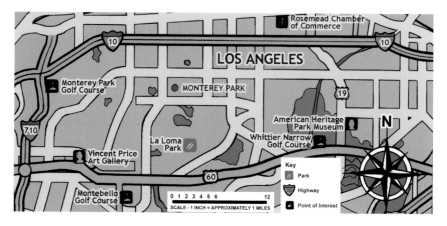

- Look at the key on this map, and read the symbols.
- Find two points of interest on the map.
- Draw a route from one point to the other.

B. Work with a partner. Write directions.

- Get a street map of your city or town.
- Find where you are on the map.
- Choose a place on the map, and write directions to drive there.
- Read your directions to the class. Show your route on the map.

Useful Expressions

It's ____ [say a number] miles/blocks from…

Go north/south/east/west.

Turn left.

Turn right.

It's near/across from…

Shared vocabulary from the *OPD*
and *Driving in the City*

OPD Link

apartment
[ə pärt**/**mənt]

bicycle
[bī**/**sĭ kəl]

confused
[kən fyōōzd**/**]

DMV clerk
[dē**/**ĕm**/**vē**/** klürk**/**]

DMV handbook
[dē**/**ĕm**/**vē**/** hănd**/**boŏk**/**]

driver's license
[drī**/**vərz lī**/**səns]

expiration date
[ĕk**/**spə rā**/**shən dāt**/**]

fire hydrant
[fīr**/** hī**/**drənt]

glad
[glăd]

OPD Link

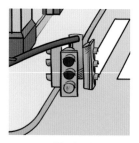

license plate
[lī/səns plāt/]

proof of insurance
[proōof/ əv/ ĭn shoōor/əns]

registration sticker
[rĕj/ə strā/shən stĭk/ər]

seat belt
[sēt/ bĕlt/]

surprised
[sər prīzd/]

testing area
[tĕs/tĭng ër/ē ə]

traffic light
[trăf/ĭk līt/]

unpack
[ŭn păk/]

vision exam
[vĭ/zhən ĭg zăm/]